Living in the Rainforest

Heather Hammonds

Chapter 1	Tropical Rainforests	2
Chapter 2	From Top to Bottom	4
Chapter 3	On the Ground	6
Chapter 4	Climbing Higher	10
Chapter 5	Up in the Treetops	14
Chapter 6	People of the Rainforest	20
Chapter 7	Living Together	22
Glossary and Index		24

Tropical Rainforests

Tropical rainforests grow in some parts of the world where it is very warm.

Many kinds of plants grow in tropical rainforests. There are tall trees and long **vines**. There are lots of beautiful flowers too.

Thousands of animals live in the rainforests. Some animals look very colourful.

Some animals look very scary!

blue morpho butterfly

tropical rainforests

bird-eating spider

3

Chapter 2

From Top to Bottom

A tropical rainforest is made up of different layers.

Some animals stay in one layer of the rainforest.

anaconda

squirrel monkey

Some animals move through all layers of the rainforest.

Layers of the Rainforest

There are several layers in the rainforest. The top layer of the rainforest is called the **emergent** layer. The middle layers are called the **canopy** and the **understorey**. The bottom layer is called the **floor**.

Emergent – the tops of the tallest trees in the rainforest.

Canopy – the green leaves and tops of most trees in the rainforest.

Understorey – tree trunks, smaller trees, vines and bushes in the rainforest.

Floor – the rainforest ground.

Chapter 3

On the Ground

Very little sunlight reaches the ground in the rainforest. The big trees block out the sun.

These ants make a huge nest under the ground. They climb into the trees and collect leaves. Then they take the leaves to their nest.

leaf-cutter ants

The ants do not eat the leaves. They keep them in their nest.

A special **fungus** grows on the leaves inside the nest. Then the ants eat the fungus.

Thousands of other insects live on the rainforest floor.

This giant centipede makes its home under old leaves and wood.

This animal lives in a cosy **burrow.** It is safe from other rainforest animals in its burrow. It eats fruit and nuts that fall from the rainforest trees.

agouti

jaguar

This big cat is a fierce hunter. It catches animals up in the trees, on the ground and in the water too.

It lives in a **den** under big trees.

Lots of other animals make their home on the rainforest floor.

This animal lives near water.

tapir

Chapter 4

Climbing Higher

Small trees and vines grow in the rainforest, not far from the ground. A little sunlight shines on this part of the rainforest, but it is still shady.

This tree frog lives on the leaves and branches of rainforest trees. It eats insects and small animals.

tree frog

These tiny bats make a tent from a leaf! At night, they fly about the rainforest. They sleep in their tent during the day. They eat fruit from the rainforest trees.

tent-making bats

poison arrow frogs

Thousands of frogs make their homes in the rainforest.

These beautiful birds fly high through the trees. They eat fruit, nuts and seeds.

They make nests for their **chicks** in **hollow** trees. The chicks stay safe inside the nest until they can fly.

Hollow trees make good homes in the rainforest.

macaws

This bird makes a nest for its chicks in a hollow tree too. It collects fruit, seeds and insects with its very long beak.

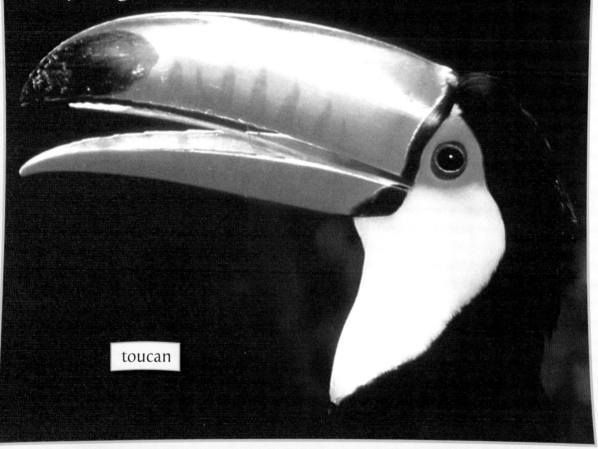

toucan

woodpeckers

Some birds make holes in rainforest trees with their beaks.

Then they make nests in the holes.

Chapter 5

Up in the Treetops

The sun shines on the treetops, high in the rainforest. There are lots of green leaves on the trees.

These monkeys live in the treetops. They make a very loud noise to keep others out of their part of the rainforest.

They eat many leaves and fruits.

howler monkeys

spider monkeys

These monkeys live in the treetops too. Each night, they sleep in a tall tree. They choose a tree that has plenty of leaves and fruit on it to eat.

Lots of different monkeys live high in the rainforest trees.

uakari

This animal makes its home in the trees. It hangs upside down, among the branches. It moves about very slowly as it looks for juicy leaves to eat.

sloth

tree boa

This tree snake makes its home in the trees too.
It does not come down to the ground very often.
It slithers through the treetops, looking for small
animals to eat.

There are many snakes in the rainforest.
Some are brightly coloured.

coral snake

Some cats live high in the rainforest trees. This small cat can climb trees very well. It hunts small animals and birds in the treetops. It makes a nest for its kittens in a hollow tree.

margay

harpy eagle

This huge bird lives in the tallest rainforest trees. It builds a nest of sticks at the top of a tree for its little chick. It hunts monkeys and other small animals, catching them in its big claws.

Many insects fly about, high in the rainforest canopy.

katydid

19

Chapter 6

People of the Rainforest

People live in the rainforest too. Some people live in **villages**, deep in the rainforest. They make small gardens around their rainforest homes to grow food.

Some people live near rivers in the rainforest. They catch fish from the rivers.

They build their homes on long poles beside the rivers.

People of the rainforest can get everything they need from the rainforest to **survive**.

Chapter 7

Living Together

More animals, insects and plants live in the rainforests than anywhere else on Earth.

Some rainforest animals and insects eat the plants and some eat other animals and insects.

People of the rainforest eat animals, plants and some insects too.

Everyone lives together in different parts of the rainforest. Tropical rainforests are very special places.

Glossary

burrow   a hole in the ground that has been dug by an animal to live in

canopy   the green leaves and tops of most trees in the rainforest

chicks   baby birds

den   a hole or a cave that is used by an animal to live in

emergent   the tops of the tallest trees in the rainforest

floor   the lowest level in the rainforest

fungus   a plant-like living thing

hollow   a big hole inside something

survive   to stay alive, or live

understorey   tree trunks, smaller trees, vines and bushes in the rainforest

villages   very small towns where groups of people live

vines   plants with long, thin stems that climb trees as they grow

Index

ants 6–7

bats 11

birds 12–13, 19

cats 9, 18

frogs 10–11

insects 7, 19, 22–23

monkeys 4, 14–15

people 20–21, 23

snakes 17